CW00687472

E

by Iain Gray

Lang**Syne**

PUBLISHING

WRITING *to* REMEMBER

LangSyne

PUBLISHING

WRITING *to* REMEMBER

79 Main Street, Newtongrange,
Midlothian EH22 4NA
Tel: 0131 344 0414
E-mail: info@lang-syne.co.uk
www.langsyneshop.co.uk

Design by Dorothy Meikle
Printed by Printwell Ltd
© Lang Syne Publishers Ltd 2022

ISBN 978-1-85217-659-4

Evans

MOTTO:
Liberty.

CREST:
A demi-lion rampant holding
a boar's head between its paws.

NAME variations include:
Evan
Evance
Evands
Evanson
Evens
Evenson
Evins

Chapter one:

Origins of Welsh surnames

by Iain Gray

If you don't know where you came from, you won't know where you're going is a frequently quoted observation and one that has a particular resonance today when there has been a marked upsurge in interest in genealogy, with increasing numbers of people curious to trace their family roots.

Main sources for genealogical research include census returns and official records of births, marriages and deaths – and the key to unlocking the detail they contain is obviously a family surname, one that has been 'inherited' and passed from generation to generation.

No matter our station in life, we all have a surname – but it was not until about the middle of the fourteenth century that the practice of being identified by a particular, or 'fixed', surname became commonly established throughout the British Isles.

Previous to this, it was normal for a person to be identified through the use of only a forename.

Wales, however, known in the Welsh language as *Cymru*, is uniquely different – with the use of what are known as patronymic names continuing well into the fifteenth century and, in remote rural areas, up until the early nineteenth century.

Patronymic names are ones where a son takes his father's forename, or Christian name, as his surname.

Examples of patronymic names throughout the British Isles include 'Johnson', indicating 'son of John', while specifically in Scotland 'son of' was denoted by the prefix Mc or Mac – with 'MacDonald', for example, meaning 'son of Donald.'

Early Welsh law, known as *Cyfraith Hywel*, *The Law of Hywel*, introduced by Hywel the Good, who ruled from Prestatyn to Pembroke between 915 AD and 950 AD, stipulated that a person's name should indicate their ancestry – the name in effect being a type of 'family tree.'

This required the prefixes *ap* or *ab* – derived from *mab*, meaning 'son of' being placed before the person's baptismal name.

In the case of females, the suffixes *verch* or *ferch*, sometimes shortened to *vch* or *vz* would be attached to their Christian name to indicate 'daughter of.'

In some cases, rather than being known for

example as *Llewellyn ap Thomas – Llewellyn son of Thomas –* Llewellyn's name would incorporate an 'ancestral tree' going back much earlier than his father.

One source gives the example of *Llewellyn ap Thomas ap Dafydd ap Evan ap Owen ap John –* meaning *Llewellyn son of Thomas son of Dafydd son of Evan son of Owen son of John.*

This leads to great confusion, to say the least, when trying to trace a person's ancestry back to a particular family – with many people having the forenames, for example, of Llewellyn, Thomas, Owen or John.

The first Act of Union between Wales and England that took place in 1536 during the reign of Henry VIII required that all Welsh names be registered in an Anglicised form – with *Hywel*, for example, becoming Howell, or Powell, and *Gruffydd* becoming Griffiths.

An early historical example of this concerns William ap John Thomas, standard bearer to Henry VIII, who became William Jones.

In many cases – as in Davies and Williams – an s was simply added to the original patronymic name, while in other cases the prefix *ap* or *ab* was contracted to *p* or *b* to prefix the name – as in *ab Evan* to form Bevan and *ap Richard* to form Pritchard.

Other original Welsh surnames – such as Morgan, originally *Morcant* – derive from ancient Celtic sources, while others stem from a person's physical characteristics – as in *Gwyn* or *Wynne* a nickname for someone with fair hair, *Gough* or *Gooch* denoting someone with red hair or a ruddy complexion, *Gethin* indicating swarthy or ugly and *Lloyd* someone with brown or grey hair.

With many popular surnames found today in Wales being based on popular Christian names such as John, this means that what is known as the 'stock' or 'pool' of names is comparatively small compared to that of common surnames found in England, Scotland and Ireland.

This explains why, in a typical Welsh village or town with many bearers of a particular name not necessarily being related, they were differentiated by being known, for example, as 'Jones the butcher', 'Jones the teacher' and 'Jones the grocer.'

Another common practice, dating from about the nineteenth century, was to differentiate among families of the same name by prefixing it with the mother's surname or hyphenating the name.

The history of the origins and development of Welsh surnames is inextricably bound up with the nation's frequently turbulent history and its rich culture.

Speaking a Celtic language known as Brythonic, which would gradually evolve into Welsh, the natives were subjected to Roman invasion in 48 AD, and in the following centuries to invasion by the Anglo-Saxons, Vikings and Normans.

Under England's ruthless and ambitious Edward I, the nation was fortified with castles between 1276 and 1295 to keep the 'rebellious' natives in check – but this did not prevent a series of bloody uprisings against English rule that included, most notably, Owain Glyndŵr's rebellion in 1400.

Politically united with England through the first Act of Union in 1536, becoming part of the Kingdom of Great Britain in 1707 and part of the United Kingdom in 1801, it was in 1999 that *Cynulliad Cenedlaethol Cymru*, the National Assembly for Wales, was officially opened by the Queen.

Welsh language and literature has flourished throughout the nation's long history.

In what is known as the Heroic Age, early Welsh poets include the late sixth century Taliesin and Aneirin, author of *Y Gododdin*.

Discovered in a thirteenth century manuscript but thought to date from anywhere between the seventh and eleventh centuries, it refers to the kingdom of Gododdin that took in south-east Scotland and

Northumberland and was part of what was once the Welsh territory known as *Hen Ogledd*, *The Old North*.

Commemorating Gododdin warriors who were killed in battle against the Angles of Bernicia and Deira at Catraith in about 600 AD, the manuscript – known as *Llyfr Aneirin*, *Book of Aneirin* – is now in the precious care of Cardiff City Library.

Other important early works by Welsh poets include the fourteenth century *Red Book of Hergest*, now held in the Bodleian Library, Oxford, and the *White Book of Rhydderch*, kept in the National Library of Wales, Aberystwyth.

William Morgan's translation of the Bible into Welsh in 1588 is hailed as having played an important role in the advancement of the Welsh language, while in 1885 Dan Isaac Davies founded the first Welsh language society.

It was in 1856 that Evan James and his son James James composed the rousing Welsh national anthem *Hen Wlad Fynhadad – Land of My Fathers*, while in the twentieth century the poet Dylan Thomas gained international fame and acclaim with poems such as *Under Milk Wood*.

The nation's proud cultural heritage is also celebrated through *Eisteddfod Genedlaethol Cymru*, the National Eisteddfod of Wales, the annual festival of music, literature and performance that is held across the nation and which traces its roots back to 1176 when Rhys ap Gruffyd, who ruled the territory of Deheubarth from 1155 to 1197, hosted a magnificent festival of poetry and song at his court in Cardigan.

The 2011 census for Wales unfortunately shows that the number of people able to speak the language has declined from 20.8% of the population of just under 3.1 million in 2001 to 19% – but overall the nation's proud culture, reflected in its surnames, still flourishes.

Many Welsh families proudly boast the heraldic device known as a Coat of Arms, as featured on our front cover.

The central motif of the Coat of Arms would originally have been what was borne on the shield of a warrior to distinguish himself from others on the battlefield.

Not featured on the Coat of Arms, but highlighted on page three, is the family motto and related crest – with the latter frequently different from the central motif.

Echoes of a far distant past can still be found in our surnames and they can be borne with pride in commemoration of our forebears.

Chapter two:

The sons of Evan

**Of Welsh origin, 'Evans' derives from the forename
'John', popularised from earliest times in various
forms throughout Christian Europe through
reverence for the Biblical St John the Baptist and
St John the Evangelist.**

Derived from the Latin 'Johannes', in turn
derived from the Hebrew 'Johonon', 'John' indicated
'God has favoured', while the Welsh form of 'Evan'
stems from 'Ifan' or 'Ieuan'.

As a patronymic name, 'Evans' derives from
'ap Evan', or 'ab Evan' – indicating 'son of Evan', with
the name Anglicised by dropping the 'ap' or 'ab' and 's'
added to denote 'son of.'

In common with many others found throughout
the British Isles today, it was popularised as a surname
in the wake of the Norman Conquest of 1066 – a pivotal
event in the history of not only England but also
of Wales, including in relation to the adoption of
surnames.

This is reflected in the famous *Domesday
Book*, a massive survey of much of England and Wales,
ordered by William the Conqueror to determine who

owned what, what it was worth and therefore how much they were liable to pay in taxes to the voracious Royal Exchequer.

Completed in 1086 and now held in the National Archives in Kew, London, 'Domesday' was an Old English word meaning 'Day of Judgement.'

This was because, in the words of one contemporary chronicler, "its decisions, like those of the Last Judgement, are unalterable."

It had been a requirement of all landholders – from the richest to the poorest – that they identify themselves for the purposes of the survey and for future reference by means of a surname.

This is why the *Domesday Book*, although written in Latin as was the practice for several centuries with both civic and ecclesiastical records, is an invaluable source for the early appearance of a wide range of surnames.

As a surname in Wales, Evans did not become firmly established until about the sixteenth century – in common with many Welsh surnames of today – but a 'John Yevans' is recorded in Monmouthshire in 1533.

Famous for landmarks that grace the landscape such as Raglan Castle, Abergavenny Castle and Tintern Abbey, it is with Monmouthshire, one of the thirteen historic Welsh counties and known in Welsh as *Sir Fynwy* – with 'Sir' denoting 'county' – that the Evans name is particularly identified.

It is a name that figures prominently in the historical record.

Recognised for his rediscovery of texts by the late sixth century poet Taliesin and Aneirin, author of *Y Gododdin*, referred to in Chapter one, Evan Evans was the priest, scholar and poet born in 1731 in Liedrod, Ceredigion.

Having attempted to establish the Welsh society *Brodoliaeth Beirdd Morganwg* – The Fraternity of Glamorgan Bards – he died in 1788, having published the acclaimed *Some Specimens of the Poetry of the Ancient Bards* twenty four years earlier.

Born in 1770 near Caernarfon, John Evans produced an early map of America's Missouri River – while it was for an extremely odd reason that he travelled to America in the first place.

An ancient legend is that Madog ap Maredudd, the last prince of the Welsh kingdom of Powys, and who died in 1160, had somehow discovered America centuries before Christopher Columbus – and there was an upsurge in interest in this in Wales in the 1790s.

The legend goes even further, claiming that there was actually a tribe of 'Welsh' Indians, descended from those who had accompanied Madog on his discovery of America.

These Welsh Indians were thought to be identified with a tribe known as the Mandan of Missouri.

Fascinated with the legend and determined to trace this mysterious tribe of Welsh descent, the bold Evans accordingly set off for America, arriving in Baltimore in 1792.

By spring of the following year he had reached St Louis, in what was then Spanish Louisiana, only to be imprisoned for a time on suspicion of being a spy.

It was not until April of 1795 that he set off to explore the Missouri River – ironically with Spanish backing.

He managed to locate the Mandan in 1796, three years before his death but, perhaps not surprisingly, he could find no trace of Welsh-speaking Indians.

His journey had not been in vain, however: having travelled 1,800 miles up the Missouri from its confluence with the Mississippi, he produced a detailed map showing the course of the river – a map subsequently used by other explorers.

From the eighteenth century to the twentieth century: Dr Gwynfor Evans was a leading light of Plaid Cymru – the Party of Wales – for thirty-six years, and the first to represent it in Parliament.

Born in 1912 in Barry, near Cardiff, his father ran a chain of shops while his mother ran a china shop.

Qualifying as a lawyer after studying at the University of Wales, Aberystwyth and St John's College, Oxford, and a fluent Welsh speaker from the age of seventeen, he had joined Plaid Cymru as a teenager.

A conscientious objector during the Second World War, he remained a pacifist throughout his life, in addition to campaigning tirelessly for Welsh independence – seeking election to Parliament on a number of occasions.

It was not until 1966, however, that he was elected for Carmarthen – the first time Plaid Cymru gained a seat in Parliament.

Losing the seat in the General Election of 1970 and failing to regain it in the election of February of 1974, he was returned again a few months later in the October election of that year.

His threat to go on hunger strike in 1980 after the Conservative government of Margaret Thatcher back-tracked on an election pledge of a Welsh language television channel, was instrumental in the government making a U-turn and the launch in November of 1982 of the Welsh channel S4C.

Failing to be re-elected in 1983, he retired from active politics and devoted his time to writing, having already penned the 1971 *It Endures* and the 1974 *Land of my Fathers: 2000 Years of Welsh History*.

He died in 2005, while there is an imposing memorial to him on the approach to Garn Goch hill fort, near Llandello and a bronze bust in Barry Library.

Chapter three:

Exploration and science

In the same mould as John Evans, who set off in search of 'Welsh' Indians, an impressive number of bearers of the Evans name have stamped their mark on the historical record as intrepid explorers.

George Evans was the surveyor born in Warwick in 1780 and who immigrated to Australia in 1802.

Appointed Surveyor General of New South Wales, he became an early explorer of the vast region – discovering the Abercrombie and Belubula River Valleys and, in 1815, becoming the first colonial explorer to enter what is now the Lachlan River Valley; he died in 1852.

Born in 1912 in Greymouth, on the South Island of New Zealand, Henry James Evans was the exploration geologist who in 1955 discovered huge deposits of the valuable mineral bauxite on the west coast of Cape York Peninsula in Northern Queensland, Australia.

Also a recipient of the President's Medal of the Australian Institute of Mining and Metallurgy for his early oil and gas exploration in Australia, he died in 1990.

Two separate bearers of the Evans name were members of Captain Robert Falcon Scott's ill-fated 1910-1913 expedition to the South Pole.

They were British naval officer Edward Evans and Petty Officer Edgar Evans: only one of them, however, was destined to return from the Antarctic.

Born in London in 1881 and having attended the Royal Naval College, Portsmouth, Edward Evans served aboard the *Morning*, the relief vessel of Scott's first Antarctic expedition – and was later invited by him to join his second expedition.

Arriving in Antarctica, he was put in charge of the motor-sledge party, but after the sledges broke down, Scott instructed him and his three-strong team to return to base camp as he and his own party continued towards the Pole.

Evans and his team made it back to base camp after a gruelling trek over the frozen wastes, and with Evans severely incapacitated by scurvy.

Petty Officer Edgar Evans, born in 1876, in Rhossili, Wales, was among the final group of five men selected by Scott for the final push to the Pole.

They reached it on January 17, 1912 – but all of them died as they attempted to return to base camp.

Edward Evans, meanwhile, was sent home in the expedition's ship *Terra Nova* in March of 1912 – but he returned the following year in command of the vessel to take off the expedition's survivors.

Promoted to the rank of commander during the First World War, it was as commander of the destroyer HMS *Broke* that in April of 1917 he successfully engaged, along with HMS *Swift*, six German destroyers that had started to bombard Dover.

In what became known as the battle of Dover Strait, at one point Evans gave the order for his destroyer to deliberately ram one of the German destroyers.

The vessels became locked together and fierce close-quarters fighting ensued before *Broke* managed to break free.

The action made Evans a national hero, while in 1928 he was promoted to Rear-Admiral commanding the Royal Australian Navy.

Created a baron, with the title Lord Mountevans of the Broke, and the author of a number of books that include *South with Scott* and a gold medallist of a number of distinguished societies including the Royal Scottish Geographical Society, he died in 1957.

Bearers of the Evans name have also excelled in the sciences.

Born in 1882 in Modesto, California, Herbert Evans was the American anatomist and embryologist who was the first to extract, from the pituitary gland,

Human Growth Hormone – essential for human growth and development.

This was after his appointment in 1915 as professor of anatomy at the University of California, Berkeley – a post he held until his death in 1971.

He was also, along with Katharine Scott Bishop, responsible for the discovery in 1922 of Vitamin E – vital for human reproduction.

Born in 1941 in Stroud, Gloucestershire, Sir Martin Evans is the leading British scientist who, in 2007, shared the Nobel Prize in Physiology or Medicine along with Mario Capecchi and Oliver Smithies.

This was for their pioneering work in 'gene targeting' – using embryonic stem cells to create specific gene modifications.

Earlier, in 1981, along with Matthew Kaufman, Evans was the first to culture embryonic stem cells from mice and cultivate them in a laboratory.

Dubbed by the media "Evans the Atom", Dr Lyn Evans, born Lyndon Evans in Aberdare in 1945, is the Welsh scientist who since 1994 has been leader of the Large Hadron Collider (LHC) project.

Built by the European Organisation for Nuclear Research, whose French abbreviation is CERN, and located on the Franco-Swiss border, the project involves complex research into particle physics and high-energy physics – particularly research into the elusive particle known as the Higgs Boson, also known as 'the God particle.'

One particularly tragic bearer of the Evans name was Timothy Evans, wrongly convicted and hanged in March of 1950 for the murder of his wife and infant child.

It subsequently emerged that the murders had been committed by John Christie, now known to have killed at least six women, including his wife, between 1943 and 1953.

Born in 1899 in Halifax, West Yorkshire, and having married and settled by the outbreak of the Second World War in a flat at 10 Rillington Place, in the Notting Hill area of London, Christie had a string of previous convictions for assault and theft – but police failed to check this before accepting him for Special Constable duties.

It was not until he moved out of 10 Rillington Place in March of 1953 that new tenants discovered the bodies of three of his victims hidden in a kitchen alcove, while others were later discovered buried in a backyard and hidden in a wash-house.

One of the bodies was identified as that of his wife, Ethel, and it was for her murder that he was hanged in July of 1953.

It subsequently emerged that some of his victims were usually strangled by Christie in his flat after he had rendered them unconscious by administering domestic gas while supposedly, in some cases, raping them – many of the unsuspecting women having come to him to obtain an abortion.

In a controversy that persists to this day, Christie had been a key prosecution witness in the trial of Welshman Timothy Evans.

Evans, born in Merthyr Tydfil, Glamorgan in 1924, and his wife Beryl had been tenants of Christie during 1948 and 1949 – and it emerged later that it was he, not Evans, who had murdered Evans' wife and infant child.

Evans was consequently granted a posthumous pardon in October of 1966, while the miscarriage of justice is considered to have significantly contributed a year before his pardon to the abolition of capital punishment for murder in the United Kingdom.

Richard Attenborough later chillingly portrayed Christie in the 1977 film *10 Rillington Place*, based in part on the book of the same name by the late campaigning journalist and author Ludovic Kennedy, while John Hurt portrayed the hapless Timothy Evans.

Chapter four:

On the world stage

The recipient of a star on the Hollywood Walk of Fame and voted a number of times one of the most beautiful women in America, Linda Evanstad is the actress better known as Linda Evans.

Of Norwegian roots through her father and born in 1942 in Hartford, Connecticut, she is best known for her role from 1981 to 1989 of Krystle Carrington in the television series *Dynasty*.

This was a role that won her an Emmy Award nomination in 1983 for Outstanding Lead Actress in a Drama.

Previously having starred from 1965 to 1969 in the television series *The Big Valley*, her other small screen credits include the *Rockford Files* and *Banacek*, while big screen credits include the 1963 *Twilight of Honour* and, from 1980, *Tom Horn*.

An actor of stage, television and film, **Clifford Evans** was born in 1902 in Caerphilly, Wales.

His many film credits include the 1941 *Love on the Dole*, the 1942 *The Foreman Went to France* and, from 1970, *One Brief Summer*; before his death in 1985, he also had roles in television series that include *The*

Prisoner, *Randall and Hopkirk (Deceased)* and *The Avengers*.

Across the Atlantic, **Chris Evans** is the American actor born in 1981 in Massachusetts.

Best known for his role of Steve Rogers – Captain America, in the 2011 *Captain America: The First Avenger* and the 2012 *The Avengers*, other screen credits include the 2001 *Not Another Teen Movie* and, from 2007, *Surfer*.

Back on British shores, **Shaun Evans**, born in Liverpool in 1980 of Northern Irish parentage, is the actor best known for his role of a young Endeavour Morse in the television detective drama series *Endeavour*.

A prequel to the *Morse* series, which starred the late John Thaw as Inspector Morse, Evans portrays Morse as a young detective constable with Oxford City Police CID.

With other television credits that include the 2002 Channel 4 comedy drama *Teachers*, the mini series *The Virgin Queen* and *Ashes to Ashes*, his big screen credits include the 2003 *The Boys from County Clare* and, from 2009, the horror film *Dread*.

Born in 1973, **Daniel Evans** is the Welsh actor whose television credits include the period dramas *Daniel Deronda* and – in common with Shaun Evans – *The Virgin Queen*, while film credits include the 1997

Be Brave, for which he was nominated for a Welsh BAFTA Award for Best Actor, and the 2012 *Les Misérables*.

Born in 1914 in Putney, London, **Edward Evans** was the British television and film actor whose big screen credits include the 1960 *The Trials of Oscar Wilde*; he died in 2001, while his television credits include *Dixon of Dock Green* and *Coronation Street*.

Apprenticed to a milliner when she was aged 15, **Dame Edith Evans** was the veteran English actress of stage and screen born in London in 1888.

Known for her roles as an aristocratic lady, she played the role on stage of Lady Bracknell in Oscar Wilde's *The Importance of Being Earnest* and also in the 1952 film of the name.

Her role in the 1963 *Tom Jones* won her an Academy Award nomination and a BAFTA for Best British Actress, as did her role in the 1967 *The Whisperers*; created a Dame Commander of the Order of the British Empire (DBE), she died in 1976.

A Welsh actor of both stage and screen, **Luke Evans** was born in 1981 in Aberbargoed, Caerphilly.

Stage roles include *Miss Saigon* – a role he reprised in the 2004 film of the name – and the 2012 *The Hobbit: An Unexpected Journey*.

Married to the 'singing cowboy' Roy Rogers,

Francis Octavia Smith was the American actress and singer better known by her stage name of **Dale Evans**.

Born in 1912 in Uvalore, Texas, it was after a highly successful radio career that she married Rogers in 1947 – the couple starring from 1951 to 1957 in the television series *The Roy Rogers Show*.

The recipient of two stars on the Hollywood Walk of Fame – one for her contribution to radio and the other for her contribution to television – she died in 2001.

Born in 1942 in Berkeley, California, **Art Evans** is the veteran American actor whose film credits include the 1990 *Die Hard 2* and whose many television credits include *M*A*S*H*, *Hill Street Blues* and *Monk*.

Returning to British shores, **Lee Evans**, born in 1964 in Avonmouth, Bristol is the stand-up comedian, actor, musician and writer whose film roles include the 1995 *Funny Bones* and the 2007 *The History of Mr Polly*.

The son of a bookmaker and a health service worker, **Chris Evans** is the English broadcaster, radio and television presenter and businessman born in 1966 in Warrington, Lancashire.

Leaving school when aged 16, he worked in a succession of jobs before joining a Manchester based radio station. Joining BBC Radio 1 in 1992, he has gone on to host a number of BBC radio programmes in addition to having worked for Virgin Radio.

His own television production company, Ginger Productions, which produced programmes such as *Don't Forget Your Toothbrush*, hosted by Evans, was sold to the Scottish Media Group (SMG) in 2000 for £225m.

The recipient in 2006 of the Music Radio Personality of the Year Award at the Sony Radio Academy Awards, he started hosting BBC Radio 2's flagship Breakfast Show in 2010.

In the world of literature, Mary Ann Evans was the great English novelist better known by her pen name of **George Eliot**.

She chose this name, she said, in order that her works would be taken seriously – works of literature at the time being perceived as the preserve of male writers.

Born in 1819 in Warwickshire, where her father was the manager of the Arbury Hall Estate of the wealthy Newdigate family, she produced seven novels.

These include the 1859 *Adam Bede*, the 1860 *The Mill on the Floss* and the 1872 *Middlemarch* – described as "one of the greatest novels in the English language."

She died in 1880, while many of her novels have since been adapted for television and film.

Named in 2000 as one of the International Press Institute's 50 World Press Freedom Heroes, **Sir Harold Evans** was born in 1928 in Newton Heath, Manchester.

The son of a railway driver, and working first for a weekly newspaper in Ashton-under-Lyne, Lancashire, he went on to edit the *Sunday Times* from 1967 to 1981.

Championing the newspaper's crusading style of journalism, it was under his editorship that it was responsible for uncovering many stories and scandals that the public would otherwise have known nothing of.

These included the scandal over the use and effects of the drug Thalidomide on children and the unmasking of former British intelligence agent Kim Philby as a Soviet spy.

Married to the American journalist Tina Brown, he has been a U.S. citizen since 1981.

A contributor to a number of news outlets and knighted for his services to journalism in 2004, he is also the author of a number of books that include his 1998 *The American Century* and its 2004 sequel *They Made America*.

From the written word to the equally creative world of music, David Howell Evans, better known as

The Edge, is the guitarist, keyboardist and backing vocalist of the Irish rock band U2.

Born in 1961 in Barking, Essex, to a Welsh family but moving as an infant to the Republic of Ireland, he became a founding member in Dublin of what would become U2.

The supporter of a number of charitable causes, in common with fellow band-mate Bono, he has enjoyed major international success with the band with albums that include their 1980 debut *Boy*, the 1987 *The Joshua Tree*, the 2004 *How to Dismantle an Atomic Bomb* the 2009 *No Line on the Horizon* and, from 2014 *Innocence*.

Two separate bearers of the name – **Dave Evans** and **Mark Evans** – have been members of the Australian hard rock band AC/DC.

Born in 1953 in Carmarthen, Wales, and later immigrating to Australia, Dave Evans was the band's original singer, from 1973 to 1974, recording with them on songs that include *Can I Sit Next to You, Girl*.

Born in Melbourne in 1956, Mark Evans is the bass guitarist who was a member of the band from 1975 to 1977 – playing on albums that include *Dirty Deeds Done Dirt Cheap* and *Let There Be Rock*.

Bearers of the Evans name have excelled in the highly competitive world of sport.

Born in 1964 in Pontarddulais, Swansea, **Ieuan**

Evans is the former rugby union player who, behind Gareth Thomas and Shane Williams, is the third highest goal scorer for Wales.

Capped 72 times for Wales and having scored 33 tries for his nation, it was when he was aged 19 and studying at Salford University that the talented wing joined Llanelli.

Leaving to join Bath in 1997, he was part of the team that won the Heineken Cup a year later.

Touring with the British and Irish Lions in 1989, 1993 and 1997, he is noted for scoring the decisive try against Australia in 1989 and captaining the team when it won the Five Nations Championship in 1994.

Retiring from the game in 1999, he is the recipient of an MBE for services to rugby and an inductee of the International Rugby Hall of Fame.

Born in Swansea in 1988, **Daniel Evans** is the Wales international rugby union fullback who has played for teams that include the Scarlets, Llanelli, Newport Gwent Dragons and the Ospreys.

From rugby to bowling, Maldwyn Evans, better known as **Mal Evans**, born in 1937 in Gelli, in the Rhondda, was the champion bowler who represented Wales from 1965 to 1983.

Winner of the world singles bowls championship in 1972 and, along with his brother Gwyn, born in 1931, the national pairs championship in 1966 and 1967, he died in 2009.

From the rugby pitch to the football pitch, **Jonny Evans**, born in Belfast in 1988, is the defender who has played for the Northern Ireland national team since 2006 and who was signed to Manchester United in 2007.

He is the brother of the midfielder **Corry Evans**, born in 1990, and who has also played for the national team and Manchester United.

One particularly inventive bearer of the proud name of Evans was the Welsh sea captain **William Evans**, born in 1790 in St Dogwells, Pembrokeshire.

Serving for a time in the Royal Navy, he invented the system of tri-coloured lighting on naval vessels to prevent collisions at sea.

For this, he was awarded £1,500 by the British government and the gift of a gold chronometer and £200 from the Russian Tsar.

He was also a highly accomplished chess player, having learned all the moves in the highly cerebral game by the age of 14 and later creating the move known in chess circles today as *Evans Gambit*.